50¢

Quote
This!

To my editor, Lizzie Brenkus. Thank you for discovering me . . . and for your patience and encouragement. You are truly missed!

Quote
This!

A Collection of
Illustrated Quotes
for Educators

Diane
HODGES

CORWIN PRESS
A SAGE Company
Thousand Oaks, CA 91320

For information:

Corwin Press
A SAGE Company
2455 Teller Road
Thousand Oaks,
  California 91320
www.corwinpress.com

SAGE India Pvt. Ltd.
B 1/I 1 Mohan Cooperative
  Industrial Area
Mathura Road,
  New Delhi 110 044
India

SAGE Ltd.
1 Oliver's Yard
55 City Road
London EC1Y 1SP
United Kingdom

SAGE Asia-Pacific Pte. Ltd.
33 Pekin Street #02-01
Far East Square
Singapore 048763

Printed in the United States of America.

Library of Congress Cataloging-in-Publication Data

Quote this!: a collection of illustrated quotes for educators/[compiled by] Diane Hodges.
  p. cm.
ISBN 978-1-4129-5785-4 (cloth w/cd)
ISBN 978-1-4129-5786-1 (paper w/cd)
  1. Education—Quotations, maxims, etc. 2. Children—Quotations. 3. Conduct of life—Quotations, maxims, etc. I. Hodges, Diane.

PN6084.E38Q69 2008
370—dc22   2007052912

This book is printed on acid-free paper.

08   09   10   11   12   10   9   8   7   6   5   4   3   2   1

Acquisitions Editor:	Arnis Burvikovs
Editorial Assistant:	Ena Rosen
Production Editor:	Cassandra Margaret Seibel
Copy Editor:	Jennifer Withers
Typesetter:	C&M Digitals (P) Ltd.
Proofreader:	Taryn Bigelow
Cover Designer:	Scott Van Atta

Contents

Preface

I am addicted to quotes. I love quotes. I collect quotes. I have an entire file cabinet that holds them, and I have moved that cabinet to three different states over the years. As I go toward the end of my career and my life, I envision my children recycling the thousands of pages in this quotes cabinet into the recycling bin. To make sure this doesn't occur, I decided to share my file cabinet with you.

I put quotes on memos, on bulletin boards, on paychecks, in restrooms . . . anywhere that I know they will be seen. I hope you will, too. I often wished that a certain quote had an illustration to accompany it that I could use in a presentation or put in the lounge. Most of the illustrations that are commercially available are for the business community, which is much different from education.

I was very fortunate to have some wonderful artists and photographers contribute to this effort and share their talents by illustrating many of the quotes. Quotes that have a 📷 next to them have an illustrative photograph on the CD that accompanies this book. Quotes with a 🎨 next to them have artwork on the CD. Please use these quotes for your own inspiration and to inspire those around you.

Finally, and most important, my most sincere thanks go to all the major artistic contributors to this book:

Elie Bernhardt graduated from San Diego State University with a BA in graphic design/illustration. Because Elie lived in Japan for four years, her art is a blend of the West and East. Her art has been published in two books and has been used as a teaching tool for young children. She works for a printing company and does freelance illustrating in San Diego.

Wendy Dickie spent the first part of her career in corporate America. She took an early retirement and is now a professional photographer. She owns Fine Eye Photography in Boulder, Colorado (www.fineeyephoto.com).

Abigail Garcia grew up in Michigan and graduated with a BFA from the University of Nevada–Las Vegas School of Art. Her art has been shown at numerous exhibitions and juried shows and at the Jefferson Underground Museum. She is the cofounder of the annual Dogtown Art Fair and lives in St. Louis, Missouri.

Patti Kenworthy is a chef and culinary arts instructor at a technology center in Michigan. Her passion for photography was ignited by taking pictures of her daughter and others during sporting events.

Steven Krasnoff is the owner of SK Financial, a residential mortgage company in San Diego. He has been painting abstract art for seven years and uses mostly oils. His passion is painting on large canvases, which allows him to expand on the emotions being conveyed through his art.

Robert Laemle is a product of the Midwest and has a degree from the University of Wisconsin in secondary education. He has been a photographer for 48 years (30 of those years as a professional photographer). For the past 28 years, he has been a senior photographer for Abbott Laboratories in Illinois. He looks forward to the "vacations" he takes through the eye of the camera lens.

Patricia Maas is a professional communications specialist and an award-winning writer, editor, and photographer. Her professional roles have included editing a national publication and serving as communications director of a large nonprofit organization. As creative director for Blue Jay Technologies, she provides Web strategy, graphic design, and custom photography services to select clientele. Some of her photography can be viewed at www.maascreative.com. Patricia holds a BA in literature from the University of California, San Diego.

Alex P. Mendoza graduated from San Diego State University with a BA and has been a graphic designer for 17 years. He has worked with Harcourt Brace Publishing, the San Diego Zoo, Warner Design, *Padre Magazine*, and *San Diego Home Garden*. Alex currently is an in-house senior designer at Sunrise Medical in Colorado.

Sarah Diane Mitchell is a freelance photographer and writer who doubles by day as a systems engineer building solar telescopes. She is originally from Paw Paw, Michigan, but now lives in San Francisco. She believes that to be happy she needs a balance between her creative and technical sides. Sarah finds that photography is "food for her soul," while science is "food for her mind."

Paige Tranbarger's love for art began at age five. Years later, she graduated from San Diego State University with a degree in graphic design and is now a freelance graphic artist in San Diego.

William Warren spent 20 years on submarines in the U.S. Navy. Following his military retirement, he became an electronics instructor at a technology center in Michigan. He is also a professional photographer and uses the camera to capture the magic that surrounds him.

Publisher's Note: While Corwin Press normally strives for inclusive language in referring to a person of nonspecified gender, the quotes in this book date back to older times and other cultures.

About the Author

Diane Hodges is the Managing Partner of Threshold Group, a consulting firm in San Diego that specializes in staff development. After more than 30 years as an educator, Diane is delighting audiences internationally with her wit and humor through her acclaimed presentation series for administrators and staff.

She served as an executive director of career and technology education, director of instructional services, director of human resources, principal, instructor, and counselor. She earned her doctorate from Michigan State University and has received 12 national and state leadership awards.

She is the best-selling author of *Looking Forward to Monday Morning* and *Looking Forward to MORE Monday Mornings*, in which she compiled ideas for recognition, appreciation, and fun things that can be done at work—all on a low budget. She is also the author of *Laugh Lines for Educators* and *Grin & Share It!*

CHAPTER ONE

Education

I dedicate myself to the life of an educator, to laying the living foundations upon which successor generations must continue to build their lives.

I dedicate myself to the advancement of learning, for I know that without it our successors will lack both the vision and the power to build well.

I dedicate myself to the cultivation of character, for I know that humanity cannot flourish without courage, compassion, honesty, and trust.

I commit myself to the advancement of my own learning and to the cultivation of my own character, for I know that I must bear witness in my own life to the ideals that I have dedicated myself to promote in others.

In the presence of this gathering, I so dedicate and commit myself.

> Steven Tigner—Affirmed annually in the Boston University
> School of Education Junior Pinning Ceremony

There is no word in the language I revere more than "teacher." My heart sings when a kid refers to me as his teacher, and it always has. I've honored myself and the entire family of man by becoming a teacher.

> Pat Conroy

Children need all school workers. A person is not "just" a janitor, not "just" a custodian. Janitors can see children when (teachers) don't see them, and bus drivers recognize that children who are disruptive on the bus are likely to be disorderly in the classroom. They're partners in education. We need each other to make this work.

> Rev. Jesse Jackson

A teacher affects eternity; he can never tell where his influence stops.

Henry B. Adams

It takes a special person with patience and wisdom to share, to unlock the treasure waiting within children everywhere.

Joan Zatorski

The future of the world is in my classroom today, a future with the potential for good or bad . . . Several future presidents are learning from me today; so are the great writers of the next decades, and so are all the so-called ordinary people who will make the decisions in a democracy. I must never forget these same young people could be the thieves and murderers of the future. Only a teacher? Thank God I have a calling to the greatest profession of all! I must be vigilant every day, lest I lose one fragile opportunity to improve tomorrow.

Ivan Welton Fitzwater

One looks back with appreciation to the brilliant teachers, but with gratitude to those who touched our human feeling. The curriculum is so much necessary raw material, but warmth is the vital element for the growing plant and for the soul of the child.

Carl Jung

Teachers can change lives with just the right mix of chalk and challenges.
~ Joyce A. Myers

Photographer: Robert O'Neil

I like to think that the greatest success of any life is the moment when a teacher touches a child's heart and it is never again the same . . . Everything America is or ever hopes to be depends upon what happens in our school's classrooms.

Frosty Troy

Any teacher can study books, but books do not necessarily bring wisdom, nor that human insight essential to consummate teaching skills.

Bliss Perry

Good teachers are like hearts . . . they will go where they are most appreciated.

Unknown

A teacher is like a candle which lights others in consuming itself.

Giovani Ruffini

What the teacher is, is more important than what he teaches.

Karl Menninger

Teachers know there will always be rocks in the road ahead of us. They will be stumbling blocks or stepping stones; it all depends on how we use them.

Unknown

 Better than a thousand days of diligent study is one day with a great teacher.

Japanese Proverb

A teacher's constant task is to take a roomful of live wires and see to it that they're grounded.

E. C. McKenzie

It is noble to teach oneself, but still nobler to teach others—and less trouble.

Mark Twain

 One hundred years from now . . . it will not matter what my bank account was, the type of house I lived in, or the kind of car I drove, but the world may be different because I was important in the life of a child.

Anonymous

To live a single day and hear a good teaching is better than to live a hundred years without knowing such teaching.

Buddha

A teacher who can arouse a feeling for one single good action, for one single good poem, accomplishes more than he who fills our memory with rows and rows of natural objects, classified with name and form.

Johann Wolfgang von Goethe

In a completely rational society, the best of us would be teach- ers and the rest of us would have to settle for something less because passing civilization along from one generation to the next ought to be the highest honor and highest responsibility anyone can have.

Lee Iacocca

A great teacher never strives to explain his vision. He simply invites you to stand beside him and see for yourself.

R. Innan

I've always tried to be aware of what I say in my films, because all of us who make motion pictures are teachers—teachers with very loud voices.

George Lucas

Compassionate teachers fill a void left by working parents who aren't able to devote enough attention to their children. Teachers don't just teach; they can be vital personalities who help young people to mature, to understand the world and to understand themselves. A good education consists of much more than useful facts and marketable skills.

Charles Platt

Teachers, I believe, are the most responsible and important members of society because their professional efforts affect the fate of the earth.

Helen Caldicott

I put the relation of a fine teacher to a student just below the relation of a mother to a son . . .

Thomas Wolfe

Teachers are the reservoirs from which, through the process of education, students draw the water of life.

Sri Sathya Sai Baba

A good teacher, like a good entertainer, first must hold his audience's attention. Then he can teach his lesson.

Hendrik John Clarke

What sculpture is to a block of marble, education is to the soul.

Joseph Addison

Teachers teach because they care. Teaching young people is what they do best. It requires long hours, patience, and care.

Horace Mann

Teachers are expected to reach unattainable goals with inadequate tools. The miracle is that at times they accomplish this impossible task.

Haim G. Ginott

Teachers who inspire know that teaching is like cultivating a garden, and those who would have nothing to do with thorns must never attempt to gather flowers.

Unknown

It takes a special person with patience and wisdom to share, to unlock the treasure waiting within children everywhere.

Joan Zatorski

Whoever first coined the phrase "you're the wind beneath my wings" most assuredly was reflecting on the sublime influence of a very special teacher.

Frank Trujillo

What greater or better gift can we offer the republic than to teach and instruct our youth.

Marcus T. Cicero

What a teacher doesn't say . . . is a telling part of what a student hears.

Maurice Natanson

You can pay people to teach, but you can't pay them to care.

Marva Collins

The dream begins, most of the time, with a teacher who believes in you, who tugs and pushes and leads you onto the next plateau, sometimes poking you with a sharp stick called truth.

Dan Rather

If a man keeps cherishing his old knowledge, so as to continuingly be acquiring new, he may be a teacher of others.

Confucius

A loving heart is the beginning of all knowledge.

Thomas Carlyle

He who dares to teach must never cease to learn.

Richard Henry Dann

We cannot hold a torch to light another's path without brightening our own.

Ben Sweetland

Education is light; lack of it is darkness.

Russian Proverb

There is a place in America to take a stand: it is public education. It is the underpinning of our cultural and political system. It is the great common ground. Public education after all is the engine that moves us as a society toward a common destiny . . . it is in public education that the American dream begins to take shape.

Tom Brokaw

Schools will change more in the next 30 years than they have since the invention of the printed book.

Peter Drucker

We can talk or dream about the glorious schools of the future or we can create them.

Marilyn Ferguson

Knowledge changes extremely fast. But that in itself is not new; knowledge has always been fast. What is new is that knowledge matters.

Peter Drucker

For the first time in human history it really matters whether or not people learn.

Peter Drucker

Education is the most important profession because through the hands of educators pass all professions.

Unknown

The most important outcome of education is to help students become independent of formal education.

Paul E. Gray

Education could be much more effective if its purpose was to ensure that by the time they leave school every boy and girl should know how much they do not know, and be imbued with a lifelong desire to know it.

William Haley

Education's purpose is to replace an empty mind with an open one.

Malcolm S. Forbes

Education that consists of learning things and not the meaning of them is feeding upon the husks and not the corn.

Mark Twain

Every time you stop a school, you will have to build a jail. What you gain at one end, you lose at the other. It's like feeding a dog on his own tail. It won't fatten the dog.

Mark Twain

There is an old saying that the course of civilization is a race between catastrophe and education. In a democracy such as ours, we must make sure that education wins the race.

John F. Kennedy

We cannot always build the future for our youth, but we can build our youth for the future.
~ Franklin D. Roosevelt

Photo from the archives of the White Lake Historical Society

There is only one thing that costs more than education today—
the lack of it.

Unknown

Education today, more than ever before, must see clearly the
dual objectives: education for living and education for making
a living.

James Mason Wood

The goal of formal education has always been to produce
people who could continue to learn on their own.

Ronald Gross

The highest result of education is tolerance.

Helen Keller

Education is the ability to listen to almost anything without los-
ing your temper.

Robert Frost

Thinking is the hardest work there is, which is the probable
reason why so few engage in it.

Henry Ford

Education is the key to unlock the golden door of freedom.

George Washington Carver

Education is a better safeguard of liberty than a standing army.

Edward Everett

Without education, you're not going anywhere in this world.

Malcolm X

Genius without education is like silver in the mine.

Benjamin Franklin

If a man empties his purse into his head, no man can take it from him. An investment in knowledge always pays the best interest.

Benjamin Franklin

Education is the movement from darkness to light.

Allan Bloom

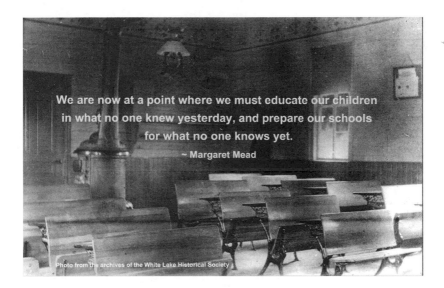

We are now at a point where we must educate our children
in what no one knew yesterday, and prepare our schools
for what no one knows yet.
~ Margaret Mead

Photo from the archives of the White Lake Historical Society

Upon the subject of education, not presuming to dictate any plan or system respecting it, I can only say that I view it as the most important subject we as people may be engaged in.

Abraham Lincoln

The most important thing about education is appetite.

Winston Churchill

The education of a man is never completed until he dies.

Robert E. Lee

Education is what survives when what has been learned has been forgotten.

B. F. Skinner

Investment in a human soul? Who knows? It might be a diamond in the rough.

Mary McLeod Bethune

The end of all education should surely be service to others.

César Chávez

Education is simply the soul of a society
as it passes from one generation to another.
~ G.K. Chesterton

Photo from the archives of the White Lake Historical Society

Education is too important to be left solely to the educators.

Francis Keppel

When I was a boy on the Mississippi River there was a proposition in a township there to discontinue public schools because they were too expensive. An old farmer spoke up and said if they stopped building the schools they would not save anything, because every time a school was closed a jail had to be built.

Mark Twain

Knowledge exists to be imparted.

Ralph Waldo Emerson

Education is for improving the lives of others and for leaving your community and world better than you found it.

Marian Wright Edelman

It is possible to store the mind with a million facts and still be entirely uneducated.

Allan Bloom

Upon the education of the people of this country
the fate of the country depends.
~ Benjamin Disraeli

Photo from the archives of the White Lake Historical Society

If you want years of prosperity, grow grain.

If you want ten years of prosperity, grow trees.

If you want one hundred years of prosperity, grow people.

Chinese Proverb

The great aim of education is not knowledge but action.

Herbert Spencer

It is not the IQ but the I WILL that is most important in education.

Unknown

The direction in which education starts a man will determine his future.

Plato

Education is a vaccine for violence.

Edward James Olmos

Education is the ability to meet life's situation.

John G. Hibben

Only the educated are free.

Epictetus

Wisdom is one treasure that no thief can touch.

Japanese Proverb

If I were asked to enumerate ten educational stupidities, the giving of grades would head the list . . . If I can't give a child a better reason for studying than a grade on a report card, I ought to lock my desk and go home and stay there.

Dorothy De Zouche

An investment in knowledge always pays the best interest.

Benjamin Franklin

Our progress as a nation can be no swifter than our progress in education. The human mind is our fundamental resource.

John F. Kennedy

Education costs money, but then so does ignorance.

Claus Moser

Creating schools for the 21st century requires less time
looking in the rear view mirror and more vision anticipating the road ahead.
- George Lucas

Photo from the archives of the White Lake Historical Society

When making a decision, ask the question "Is it good for kids?" If the response is "yes," then you have your answer.

Diane Hodges

Much that passes for education . . . is not education at all but ritual. The fact is that we are being educated when we know it least.

David P. Gardner

Knowledge—like the sky—is never private property . . . teaching is the art of sharing.

Abraham Joshua Heschel

It is the supreme art of the teacher to awaken joy in creative expression and knowledge.

Albert Einstein

Let us think of education as the means of developing our greatest abilities, because in each of us there is a private hope and dream which, fulfilled, can be translated into benefit for everyone and greater strength for our nation.

John F. Kennedy

The whole art of teaching is only the art of awakening the natural curiosity of young minds for the purpose of satisfying it afterwards.

Anatole France

The job of the teacher is to teach students to see the vitality in themselves.

Joseph Campbell

In teaching children we must seek insensibly to unite knowledge with the carrying out of that knowledge into practice.

Immanuel Kant

The art of teaching is the art of assisting discovery.

Mark Van Doren

Education to be successful must not only inform but inspire.

T. Sharper Knowlson

Real education should consist of drawing the goodness and the best out of our own students. What better books can there be than the book of humanity?

César Chávez

Teach others NOT what you have learned, BUT what you are learning.

Craig Pace

I teach with my heart and my soul and not with my mouth alone.

Jaime Escalante

Be all that you can be. Find your future—as a teacher.

Madeline Fuchs Holzer

The mediocre teacher tells. The good teacher explains. The superior teacher demonstrates. The great teacher inspires.

William Arthur Ward

It's never enough to just tell people about some new insight. Rather, you have to get them to experience it in a way that evokes its power and possibility. Instead of pouring knowledge into people's hands, you need to help them grind a new set of eyeglasses so they can see the world in a new way.

John Seely Brown

I care not what subject is taught, if only it be taught well.

T. H. Huxley

The object of teaching a child is to enable him to get along without his teacher.

Elbert Hubbard

Treat a man as he is and he will remain as he is. Treat a man as he can and should be and he will become as he can and should be.

Johann Wolfgang von Goethe

The secret of teaching is to appear to have known all your life what you learned this afternoon.

Unknown

Spoon feeding in the long run teaches us nothing but the shape of the spoon.

E. M. Forster

In seeking knowledge, the first step is silence, the second listening, the third remembering, the fourth practicing, and the fifth—teaching others.

Solomon Ibn Gabirol

A teacher's day is one-half bureaucracy, one-half crisis, one-half monotony, and one-eighth epiphany. Never mind the arithmetic.

Susan Ohanian

Good teachers never say anything. What they do is create the conditions under which learning takes place.

S. I. Hayakawa

Education is not filling a bucket but lighting a fire.

William Butler Yeats

Children have to be educated, but they also have to be left to educate themselves.

Ernest Dimnet

If a child can't learn the way we teach, maybe we should teach the way they learn.

Ignacio Estrada

The most important thing is not so much that every child should be taught, as that every child should be given the wish to learn.

John Lubbock

Those who educate children well are more honored than parents, for these only gave life, those the art of living well.

Aristotle

Do not train a child to learn by force or harshness; but direct them to it by what amuses their minds, so that you may be better able to discover with accuracy the peculiar bent of the genius of each.

Plato

The best teachers teach from the heart, not from the book.

Unknown

 I do not teach. I relate.

Michel de Montaigne

Example isn't another way to teach, it is the only way to teach.

Albert Einstein

How to tell students what to look for without telling them what to see is the dilemma of teaching.

Lascelles Abercrombie

The beauty of empowering others is that your own power is not diminished in the process.

Barbara Colorose

If a doctor, lawyer, or dentist had forty people in his office at one time, all of whom had different needs, and some of whom didn't want to be there and were causing trouble, and the doctor, lawyer, or dentist, without assistance, had to treat them all with professional excellence for nine months, then he might have some conception of the classroom teacher's job.

Donald D. Quinn

Good teaching is one-fourth preparation and three-fourths theater.

Gail Godwin

A teacher is one who makes himself progressively unnecessary.

Thomas Carruthers

Don't try to fix the students, fix ourselves first. The good teacher makes the poor student good and the good student superior. When our students fail, we, as teachers, too, have failed.

Marva Collins

I like the teacher that gives you something to take home to think about besides homework.

Lily Tomlin as "Edith Ann"

In teaching you cannot see the fruit of a day's work. It is invisible and remains so, maybe for twenty years.

Jacques Barzun

You cannot teach a man anything; you can only help him find it within himself.

Galileo

Teaching was the hardest work I have ever done . . .

Ann Richards

Too often we give our children answers to remember rather than problems to solve.

Roger Lewin

Teach to the problems, not to the text.

E. Kim Nebeuts

Teachers open the door, but you must enter by yourself.

Chinese Proverb

Minds are like parachutes—they only function when open.

Thomas Dewar

Learning is by nature curiosity.

Philo

Free the child's potential, and you will transform him into the world.

Maria Montessori

Human beings strive for understanding and mastery, and tend to be motivated when they effectively learn something they value.

Raymond Wlodkowski

The mind is not a vessel to be filled, but a fire to be ignited.

Plutarch

When you are through learning, you're through.

Vernon Law

The most beautiful thing about learning is that no one can take it away from you.

B. B. King

Live as if you were to die tomorrow. Learn as if you were to live forever.

Mahatma Gandhi

 He who would learn to fly one day must first learn to stand and walk and run and climb and dance; one cannot fly into flying.

Friedrich Nietzsche

I hear, and I forget. I see, and I remember. I do, and I understand.

Chinese Proverb

I forget what I was taught. I only remember what I have learned.

Patrick White

The focus of learning will shift from schools to employers.

Peter Drucker

Learning is finding out what you already know,

Doing is demonstrating that you know it,

Teaching is reminding others that they know it as well as you do.

We are all learners, doers, and teachers.

Richard Bach

Life does not consist mainly, or even largely, of facts and happenings. It consists mainly of the storm of thought that is forever flowing through one's head.

Mark Twain

Experience is a hard teacher because she gives the test first, and the lesson afterward.

Vernon Law

Man's mind, once stretched by a new idea, never regains its original dimensions.

Oliver Wendell Holmes

Never stop learning; knowledge doubles every fourteen months.

Anthony J. D'Angelo

Invest in yourself, in your education. There's nothing better.

Sylvia Porter

 Not I, but the city teaches.

Socrates

Where did we ever get the crazy idea that in order to make people do better, first we must make them feel worse? Think of the last time you felt humiliated or treated unfairly. Did you feel like cooperating or doing better?

Jane Nelson

 The most effective kind of education is that a child should play amongst lovely things.

Unknown

 Today a reader, tomorrow a leader.

Margaret Fuller

Think left and think right and think low and think high. Oh, the thinks you can think up if you only try!

Dr. Seuss

There is more treasure in books than in all the pirate's loot on Treasure Island.

Walt Disney

The more that you read, the more things you will know. The more that you learn, the more places you'll go.

Dr. Seuss

To learn to read is to light a fire; every syllable that is spelled out is a spark.

Victor Hugo

Nature and books belong to the eyes that see them.

Ralph Waldo Emerson

America's future walks through the doors of our schools each day.

Mary Jean Le Tendre

Students are volunteers, whether we want them to be or not. Their attendance can be commanded, but their attention must be earned. Their compliance can be insisted upon, but their commitment is under their own control.

Phillip Schlechty

I consider a human soul without education like marble in a quarry, which shows none of its inherent beauties until the skill of the polisher sketches out the colors, makes the surface shine, and discovers every ornamental cloud, spot, and vein that runs through it.

Joseph Addison

 There is a brilliant child locked inside every student.

Marva Collins

 We worry about what a child will become tomorrow, yet we forget that he is someone today.

Stacia Tauscher

 Every child is born a genius.

Albert Einstein

A child miseducated is a child lost.

John F. Kennedy

 All children have creative power.

Brenda Ueland

It is important that students bring a certain ragamuffin, bare-foot irreverence to their studies; they are not here to worship what is known, but to question it.

Jacob Bronowski

Everyone is ignorant, only on different subjects.

Will Rogers

It is not the strongest of the species that survives, nor the most intelligent, but the one most responsive to change.

Charles Darwin

The only person who is educated is the one who has learned how to learn and change.

Carl Rogers

CHAPTER TWO

Children

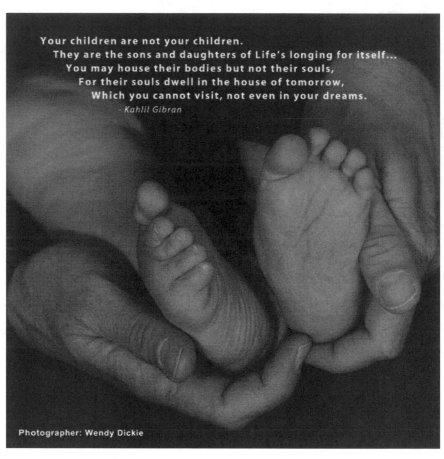

Your children are not your children.
They are the sons and daughters of Life's longing for itself...
You may house their bodies but not their souls,
For their souls dwell in the house of tomorrow,
Which you cannot visit, not even in your dreams.

- Kahlil Gibran

Photographer: Wendy Dickie

Let us put our minds together and see what life we can make for our children.

Sitting Bull

Children are one-third of our population and all of our future.

Select Panel for the Promotion of Child Health

Children are the only future of any people.

Frances Cress Welsing

We know that the outcast and misfits are the children most likely to become violent, so it only follows that we must pull them into the arms of love and/or acceptance, and find a place where they fit. If our system doesn't have a place where a child fits, there's something wrong with the system, not the child.

William DeFoore

Children are the world's most valuable resource and its best hope for the future.

John F. Kennedy

Where children are, there is the golden age.

Novalis

Children are the living messages we send to a time we will not see.

John W. Whitehead

One generation plants the trees; another gets the shade.

Chinese Proverb

If you want your children to improve, let them overhear the nice things you say about them.

Haim G. Ginott

In short, the habits we form from childhood make no small difference, but rather they make all the difference.

Aristotle

My mother and I could always look outside the same window without ever seeing the same thing.

Gloria Swanson

There is always a moment in
childhood when the door opens
and lets the future in.

–Graham Greene

Model: Nicholas A. Bernstein

CHILDREN ARE APT TO LIVE UP TO
WHAT YOU BELIEVE OF THEM.

–Lady Bird Johnson

The function of the child is to live his own life—not live the life that his anxious parents think he should live.

A. S. Neil

The child must know that he is a miracle, that since the beginning of the world there hasn't been, and until the end of the world will not be, another child like him.

Pablo Casals

To value his own good opinion, a child has to feel he is a worthwhile person. He has to have confidence in himself as an individual.

Sidonie Gruenberg

Self-esteem is the real magic wand that can form a child's future. A child's self-esteem affects every area of her existence, from friends she chooses, to how well she does academically in school, to what kind of job she gets, to even the person she chooses to marry.

Stephanie Marston

All kids need a little help, a little hope, and somebody who believes in them.

Earvin "Magic" Johnson

Children need love, especially when they do not deserve it.

Harold Hulbert

Pretty much all of the honest truth-telling there is in the world is done by children.

Oliver Wendell Holmes

While we try to teach our children all about life, our children teach us what life is all about.

Angela Schwindt

You can learn many things from children. How much patience you have, for instance.

Franklin P. Adams

Children have never been very good at listening to adults but they have never failed to imitate them.

James Baldwyn

Childhood is the most beautiful of all life's seasons.

Unknown

Many things we need can wait; the child cannot. Now is the time his bones are being formed, his blood being made, his mind being developed. To him, we cannot say, tomorrow. His name is today.

Gabriela Mistral

Be gentle with the young.

Juvenal

The best inheritance a person can give to his children is a few minutes of his time each day.

O. A. Battista

Children have more need of models than critics.

Joseph Joubert

Children need your presence more than your presents.

Rev. Jesse Jackson

Give love to a child, and you get a great deal back.

John Ruskin

The child who acts unlovable is the child who most needs to be loved.

Cathy Rindner Tempelsman

The child benefits more from being valued than evaluated.

Don Dinkmeyer

Children make you want to start life over again.

Muhammad Ali

There is a garden in every childhood, an enchanted place where colors are brighter, the air softer, and the morning more fragrant than ever again.

Elizabeth Lawrence

The brightest light, the light of Italy, the purest sky of Scandinavia in the month of June is only a half-light when one compares it to the light of childhood. Even the nights were blue.

Eugène Ionesco

When I grow up, I want to be a little girl.

Diane Hodges

The older I grow the more earnestly I feel the few joys of childhood are the best that life has to give.

Ellen Glasgow

Do not handicap your children by making their lives too easy.

Robert Heinlein

If you want children to keep their feet on the ground, put some responsibility on their shoulders.

Abigail Van Buren

The more we shelter children from every disappointment, the more devastating future disappointments will be.

Fred Gosman

A child building a sandcastle is not "working hard." It doesn't seem to him to be a task. It simply fills his imagination . . .

Jonathan Miller

Children's games are hardly games. Children are never more serious than when they play.

Michel de Montaigne

The greatest natural resource is the minds of our children.

Walt Disney

The older I get, the more I marvel at the wisdom of children.

David Morgan

TRULY
WONDERFUL
THE MIND
OF A CHILD
IS.

- YODA,
STAR WARS

Photographer: Wendy Dickie

Allow children to be happy in their own way, for what better way will they find?

Samuel Johnson

Our children are watching us live, and what we ARE shouts louder than anything we say.

Wilferd A. Peterson

 There are no seven wonders of the world in the eyes of a child. There are seven million.

Walt Streightiff

All children are artists. The problem is how to remain an artist once he grows up.

Pablo Picasso

When I was a child, my mother said to me, "If you become a soldier, you'll be a general. If you become a monk you'll end up as the pope." Instead I became a painter and wound up as Picasso.

Pablo Picasso

If children grew up according to early indications, we should have nothing but geniuses.

Johann Wolfgang von Goethe

There are perhaps no days of our childhood we lived so fully as those we spent with a favorite book.

Marcel Proust

One of the greatest gifts adults can give—to their offspring and to their society—is to read to children.

Carl Sagan

There are only two lasting bequests we can give our children. One of these is roots; the other, wings.

Hodding Carter

Children are like wet cement. Whatever falls on them makes an impression.

Haim G. Ginott

Nothing you do for children is ever wasted. They seem not to notice us, hovering, averting our eyes, and they seldom offer thanks, but what we do for them is never wasted.

Garrison Keillor

There are many little ways to
enlarge your child's world.
Love of books is best of all.

– Jacqueline Kennedy

Model: Nicholas A. Bernstein

CHAPTER THREE

Leadership

In the battle that goes on for life

I ask for a field that is fair,

A chance that is equal with all in strife,

The courage to do and to dare.

If I should win, let it be by the code,

My faith and honor held high.

If I should lose, let me stand by the road

And cheer as the winner goes by.

Knute Rockne

Leadership is action, not position.

Donald H. McGannon

I have learned that success is to be measured not by the position that one has reached in life as by obstacles which he has overcome while trying to succeed.

Booker T. Washington

An army of a thousand is easy to find, but, ah, how difficult to find a general.

Chinese Proverb

WE WILL BE KNOWN FOREVER
BY THE TRACKS WE LEAVE

– *Dakota*

Drawing by: Alex P. Mendoza

The sea is so wide and my boat is so small.

Breton Fisherman's Prayer

Know what you want to do, hold the thought firmly, and do every day what should be done, and every sunset will see you that much nearer the goal.

Elbert Hubbard

The leaders who work most effectively, it seems to me, never say "I." And that's not because they have trained themselves not to say "I." They don't think "I." They think "we"; they think "team." They understand their job to be to make the team function. They accept responsibility and don't sidestep it, but "we" gets the credit . . . This is what creates trust, what enables you to get the task done.

Peter Drucker

The desire to reach for the sky runs deep in our human psyche.

Cesar Pelli

Leadership is . . .

Courage to adjust mistakes,

Vision to welcome change, and

Confidence to stay out of step when everyone else is marching to the wrong tune!

Patty Hendrickson

Some succeed because they are destined to, but most succeed because they are determined to.

Unknown

Fairness is the art of ruffling feathers without ruining anybody's hair-do.

Gerhard Bronner

Do not go where the path may lead; go instead where there is no path and leave a trail.

Ralph Waldo Emerson

It is a rough road that leads to the heights of greatness.

Seneca

You can't direct the wind, but you can adjust the sails.

Christophe Poizat

If you don't know where you are going, any road will take you there.

Lewis Carroll

A good plan is like a road map: it shows the final destination and usually the best way to get there.

H. Stanley Judd

Success depends upon previous preparation, and without such preparation there is sure to be failure.

Confucius

When all's said and done, all roads lead to the same end. So, it's not so much which road you take, as how you take it.

Charles de Lint

No one can persuade another to change. Each of us guards a gate of change that can only be opened from the inside. We cannot open the gate of another either by argument or emotional appeal.

Marilyn Ferguson

A ship in harbor is safe—but that is not what ships are for.

John A. Shedd

Loyalty to a petrified opinion never yet broke a chain or freed one human soul—and it never will.

Mark Twain

Leaders don't force people to follow—they invite them on the journey.

Charles S. Lauer

Set your sights high, the higher the better. Expect the most wonderful things to happen, not in the future, but right now. Realize that nothing is too good. Allow absolutely nothing to hamper you or hold you up in any way.

Eileen Caddy

Leadership is the special quality which enables people to stand up and pull the rest of us over the horizon.

James L. Fisher

 To realize one's destiny is a person's only obligation . . . and when you want something, all the universe conspires in helping you to achieve it.

Paul Coelho

Make the most of yourself, for that is all there is of you.

Ralph Waldo Emerson

Whenever ideas are shared, the result is always greater than the sum of the parts.

Rich Willis

Don't tell people how to do things, tell them what to do and let them surprise you with their results.

George S. Patton

If you're not failing every now and again, it's a sure sign that you're not trying anything innovative.

Woody Allen

What would you attempt to do if you knew you could not fail?

Robert H. Schuller

If you get up one more time than you fall, you will make it through.

Chinese Proverb

Keep your fears to yourself, but share your inspiration with others.

Robert Louis Stevenson

You can dream, create, design, and build the most wonderful place in the world, but it requires people to make the dream a reality.

Walt Disney

If your actions inspire others to dream more, learn more, do more, and become more, you are a leader.

John Quincy Adams

You do not lead by hitting people over the head—that's assault, not leadership.

Dwight D. Eisenhower

A leader takes people where they want to go. A great leader takes people where they don't necessarily want to go, but ought to be.

Rosalynn Carter

My grandfather once told me that there were two kinds of people: those who do the work and those who take the credit. He told me to try to be in the first group. There is much less competition.

Indira Gandhi

Management is doing things right; leadership is doing the right things.

Peter Drucker

The only place where success comes before work is in the dictionary.

Vidal Sassoon

That man is successful who has lived well, laughed often, and loved much; who has gained the respect of the intelligent men and the love of children; who has filled his niche and accomplished his task; who leaves the world better than he found it, whether by an improved poppy, a perfect poem, or a rescued soul; who never lacked appreciation of earth's beauty or failed to express it; who looked for the best in others and gave the best he had.

Robert Louis Stevenson

Always do what you are afraid of doing.

Ralph Waldo Emerson

Whatever made you successful in the past won't in the future.

Lew Platt

Man cannot discover new oceans unless he has the courage to lose sight of the shore.

André Gide

To swear off making mistakes is very easy. All you have to do is swear off having ideas.

Leo Burnett

The biggest job we have to teach a newly hired employee is how to fail intelligently. We have to train him to experiment over and over and to keep on trying and failing until he learns what will work.

Charles F. Kettering

Ideas won't keep; something has to be done with them.

Alfred North Whitehead

If nothing ever changed, there'd be no butterflies.

Unknown

When you have exhausted all possibilities, remember this. You haven't.

Thomas Edison

If everybody is thinking alike, then somebody isn't thinking.

George S. Patton

The best way to predict the future is to invent it.

Alan Kay

We all live under the same sky, but we don't all have the same horizon.

Konrad Adenauer

Be the change you wish the world to see.

Mahatma Gandhi

You will miss 100% of the shots you don't take.

Wayne Gretzky

People don't care how much you know until they know how much you care.

John C. Maxwell

Fail to plan, plan to fail.

Carl Buechner

To praise is an investment in happiness.

George M. Adams

I praise loudly, I blame softly.

Catherine the Great

A word of encouragement during a failure is worth more than an hour of praise after success.

Unknown

The sweetest of all sounds is praise.

Xenophon

The speed of the leader determines the rate of the pack.

Wayne Lukas

If you refuse to accept anything but the best, you very often get it.

W. Somerset Maugham

Waiting until everything is perfect before making a move is like waiting to start a trip until all the traffic lights are green.

Karen Ireland

The greater the obstacle, the more glory in overcoming it.

Molière

If a man does not know to what port he is steering, no wind is favorable to him.

Seneca

 A man is a lion in his own cause.

Scottish Proverb

A lion sleeps in the heart of every brave man.

Turkish Proverb

An army of sheep led by a lion would defeat an army of lions led by a sheep.

Arab Proverb

 Good timber does not grow with ease; the stronger the wind, the stronger the trees.

J. Willard Marriott

CHAPTER FOUR

Human/Work Relations

We could all learn a lot from crayons:

Some are sharp,

Some are pretty,

Some are dull,

Some have weird names,

And all are different colors . . .

But they all have learned to live in the same box.

Unknown

Thousands of candles can be lit from a single candle, and the life of the candle will not be shortened. Happiness never decreases by being shared.

Buddha

The door to happiness opens outward.

Unknown

Remember what Bilbo used to say, "It's dangerous business, Frodo, going out your door. You step onto the road, and if you don't keep your feet, there's no knowing where you might be swept off to."

J. R. R. Tolkien

Bloom where you are planted.

Mary Engelbreit

Some people are always grumbling because roses have thorns. I am thankful that thorns have roses.

Alphonse Karr

I have always plucked a thistle and planted a flower where I thought a flower would grow.

Abraham Lincoln

Always put yourself in others' shoes. If you feel it hurts, it will probably hurt the other person, too.

Unknown

Even a fish wouldn't get into trouble if it kept its mouth shut.

Korean Proverb

A good sense of humor is essential to deal with the world's reality.

Unknown

I have seen what a laugh can do. It can transform almost unbearable tears into something bearable, even hopeful.

Bob Hope

 Laughter is an instant vacation.

Milton Berle

Carry laughter with you wherever you go.

Hugh Sidey

 A laugh is a smile that bursts.

Ralph Waldo Emerson

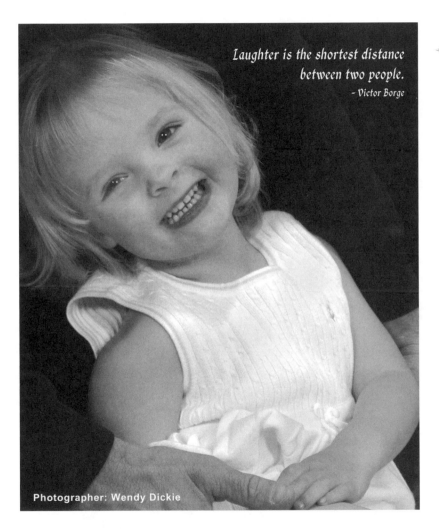

Laughter is the shortest distance between two people.
- Victor Borge

Photographer: Wendy Dickie

Laughter is
the tonic, the relief,
the surcease for pain.

– *Charlie Chaplin*

Artist: Alex P. Mendoza

A warm smile is the universal language of kindness.

William Arthur Ward

Life is short—break the rules

Forgive quickly

Laugh uncontrollably

And never forget anything that made you smile.

Unknown

We shall never know all the good that a simple smile can do.

Mother Teresa

Dreams are where we're going; work is how we get there.

Unknown

Let yourself be open and life will be easier. A spoon of salt in a glass of water makes the water undrinkable. A spoon of salt in a lake is almost unnoticed.

Buddha

I find it fascinating that most people plan their vacations with better care than they plan their lives. Perhaps that is because escape is easier than change.

Jim Rohn

 Nobody can be uncheered with a balloon.

Winnie the Pooh

 Look at everything as though you were seeing it either for the first or last time.

Betty Smith

Enjoy the little things, for one day you may look back and realize they were big things.

Robert Brault

 Think big thoughts but relish small pleasures.

H. Jackson Brown, Jr.

A CHILD REMINDS US THAT PLAYTIME IS AN ESSENTIAL PART OF OUR DAILY ROUTINE.

- ANONYMOUS

Photographer: Wendy Dickie

The shoe that fits one person pinches another;

there is no recipe for living that fits all cases.
-Carl Jung

Artist: Paige Tranberger

I learned what is obvious to a child. That life is simply a collection of little lives, each lived one day at a time. That each day should be spent in flowers and poetry and talking to animals. That a day spent with dreaming and sunsets and refreshing breezes cannot be bettered.

Nicholas Sparks

We should know that we are all part of the whole, we are all together. And everything that we do affects each other.

Yoko Ono

Individual commitment to a group effort—that is what makes a team work, a company work, a society work, a civilization work.

Vince Lombardi

Snowflakes are one of nature's most fragile things, but just look what they can do when they stick together.

Vesta M. Kelly

And it is still true,
no matter how old you are,
when you go out in the world,
it is best to hold hands
and stick together.

- Robert Fulghum
All I Really Need to Know
I Learned in Kindergarten

Photographer: Wendy Dickie

The world is full of cactus, but we don't have to sit on it.

Will Foley

Look deep into nature, and then you will understand everything better.

Albert Einstein

The only disability in life is a bad attitude.

Scott Hamilton

Don't go around saying the world owes you a living; the world owes you nothing; it was here first.

Mark Twain

Never cut a tree down in the wintertime. Never make a negative decision in the low time. Never make your most important decisions when you are in your worst moods. Wait. Be patient. The storm will pass. The spring will come.

Robert H. Schuller

When you find peace within yourself, you become the kind of person who can live at peace with others.

Peace Pilgrim

No one can make you feel inferior without your consent.

Eleanor Roosevelt

 To live through a period of stress and sorrow with another human being creates a bond which nothing seems able to break. People can be happy together and look back on their contacts very pleasantly, but such contacts will not make the same bond that sorrow lived through will create.

Eleanor Roosevelt

 Wherever you go, no matter what the weather, always bring your own sunshine.

Anthony J. D'Angelo

 The world is a rose; smell and pass it on to friends.

Persian Proverb

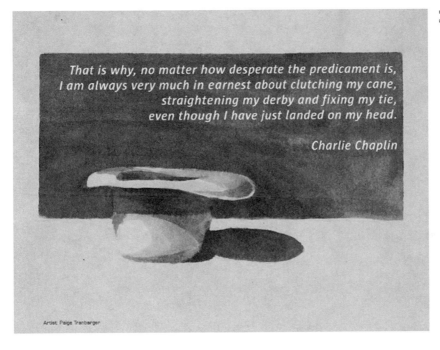

That is why, no matter how desperate the predicament is,
I am always very much in earnest about clutching my cane,
straightening my derby and fixing my tie,
even though I have just landed on my head.

Charlie Chaplin

Artist: Paige Tranbarger

There is more hunger for love
and appreciation
in this world than for bread.

- Mother Teresa

Photographer: Wendy Dickie

One kind word can warm three winter months.

Japanese Proverb

Photo by: WR Warren

Go confidently in the direction of your dreams. Live the life you have always imagined.

Henry David Thoreau

 A helping word to one in trouble is often like a switch on a railroad track . . . an inch between wreck and smooth, rolling prosperity.

Henry Ward Beecher

 Praise is like sunlight to the human spirit: we cannot flower and grow without it.

Jesse Lair

 Sticks and stones may break your bones, but words cause permanent damage.

Barry Champlain

 As the ocean is never full of water, so is the heart never full of love.

Unknown

You can't stand in your corner of the forest waiting for others to come to you. You have to go to them sometimes.

Winnie the Pooh

Love everyone as you do your dog.

Diane Hodges

True friendship is seen through the heart, not through the eyes.

Unknown

The bitterest tears shed over graves are the words left unsaid and deeds left undone.

Harriet Beecher Stowe

The smallest good deed is better than the grandest good intention.

Duguet

The first duty of love...

is to listen.
- Paul Tillich

Photographer: Wendy Dickie

Like what you do. If you don't like it, do something else.

Paul Harvey

Your chances of success are directly proportional to the degree
of pleasure you derive from what you do. If you are in a job
you hate, face the fact squarely and get out.

Michael Korda

If you don't get a kick out of the job you're doing, you'd better
hunt for another one.

Samuel Vauclain

It is what we do easily and what we like to do that we do well.

Orison Swett Marden

I never did a day's work in my life. It was all fun.

Thomas Edison

Work is love made visible.

Kahlil Gibran

 Find your passion and have the courage to pursue it.

Lawrence Bacow

 Find the seed at the bottom of your heart and bring forth a flower.

Shigenori Kameoka

 Keep a tree in your heart and perhaps a singing bird will come.

Chinese Proverb

 Where flowers bloom so does hope.

Lady Bird Johnson

We need quiet time to examine our lives openly and honestly . . . spending quiet time alone gives your mind an opportunity to renew itself and create order.

Susan L. Taylor

Rivers know this: there is no hurry. We shall get there some day.

Winnie the Pooh

You can't stop the waves, but you can learn to surf.

Jon Kabat-Zinn

What is life?

It is the flash of a firefly in the night.

It is the breath of a buffalo in the wintertime.

It is the little shadow which runs across the grass and loses itself in the sunset.

Crowfoot

Sometimes our fate resembles a fruit tree in winter. Who would think that those branches would turn green again and blossom, but we hope it, we know it.

Johann Wolfgang von Goethe

Keep your face to the sunshine and you cannot see a shadow.

Helen Keller

Live that you wouldn't be ashamed to sell the family parrot to the town gossip.

Will Rogers

CORWIN PRESS

The Corwin Press logo—a raven striding across an open book—represents the union of courage and learning. Corwin Press is committed to improving education for all learners by publishing books and other professional development resources for those serving the field of PreK–12 education. By providing practical, hands-on materials, Corwin Press continues to carry out the promise of its motto: **"Helping Educators Do Their Work Better."**